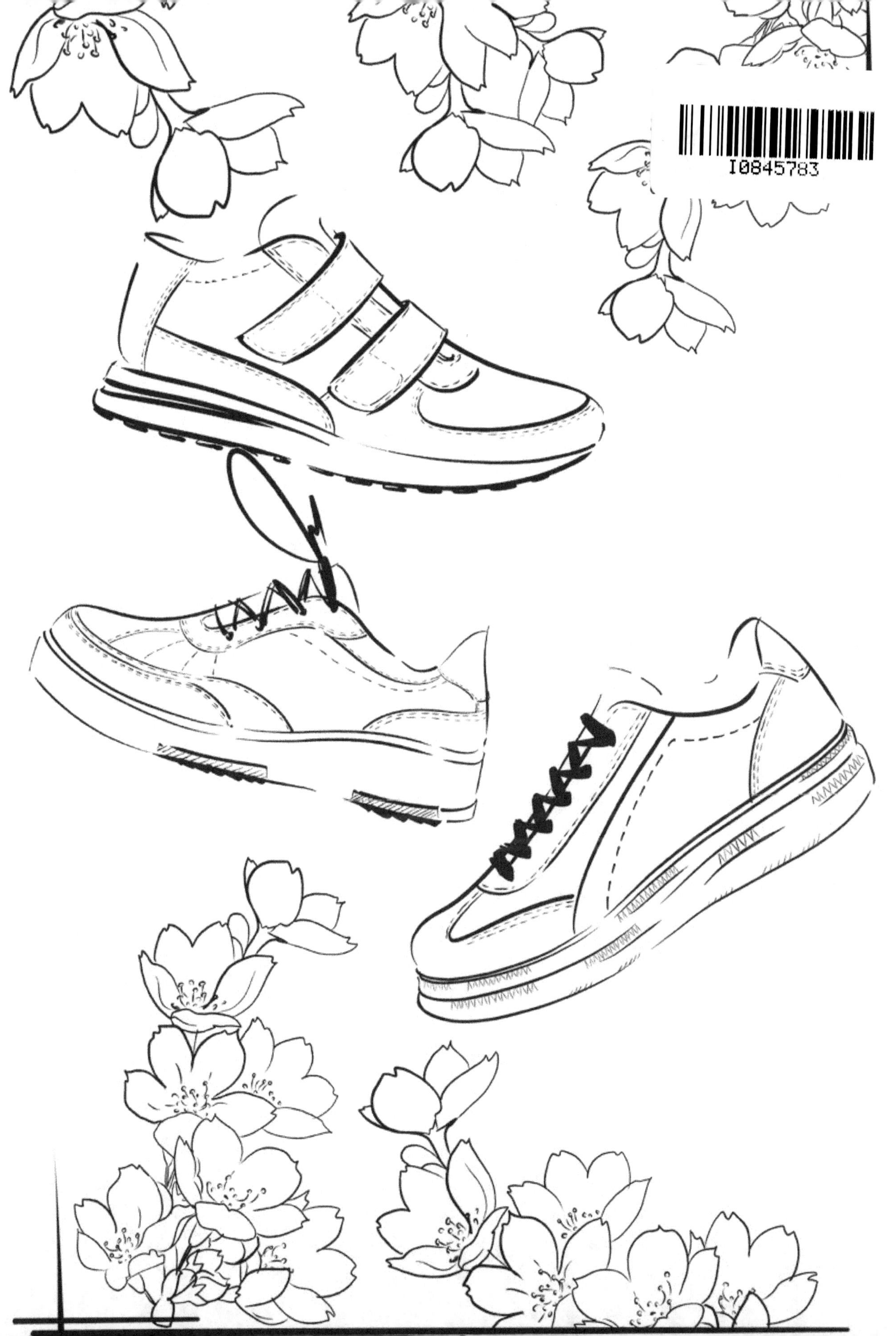

I0845783

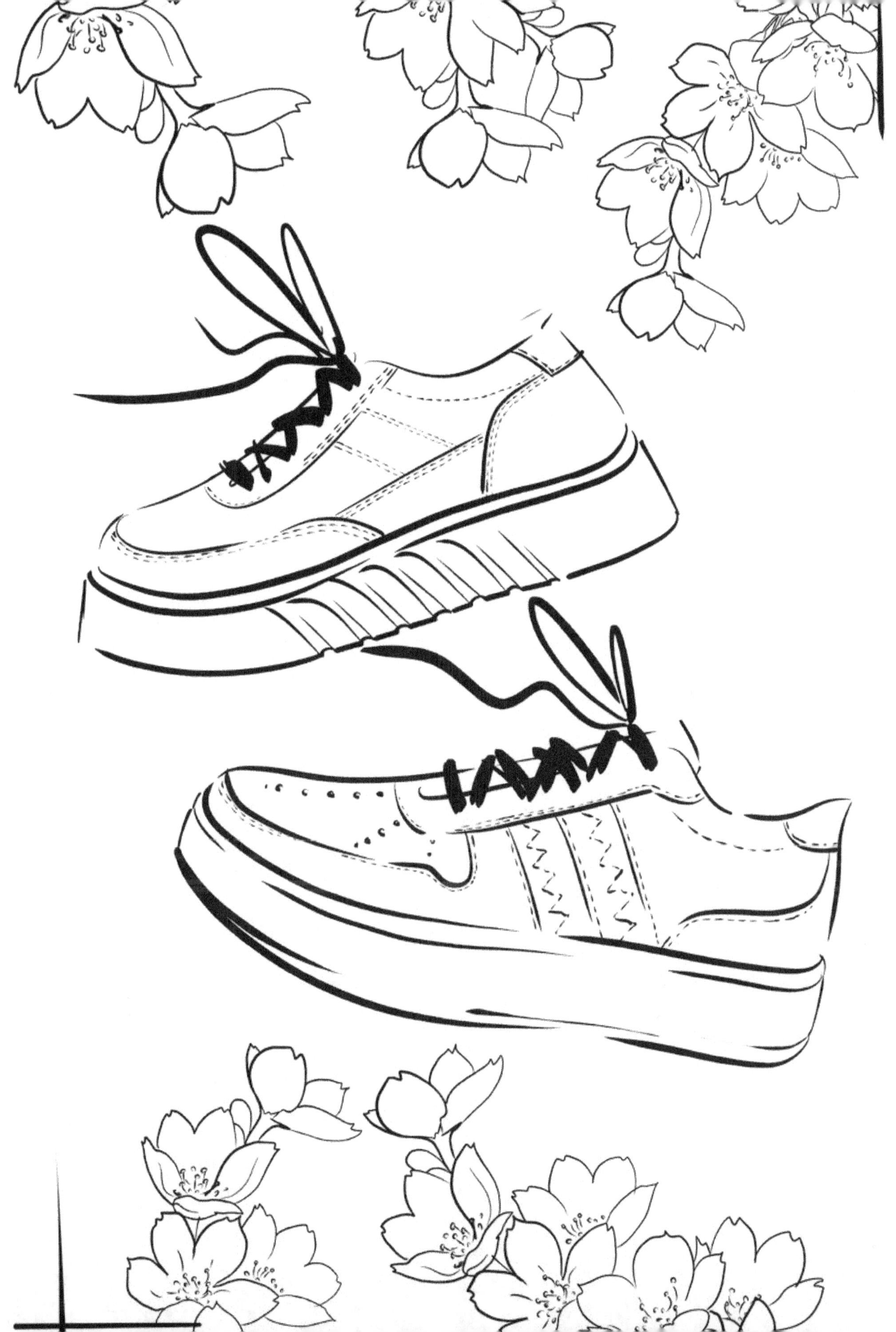

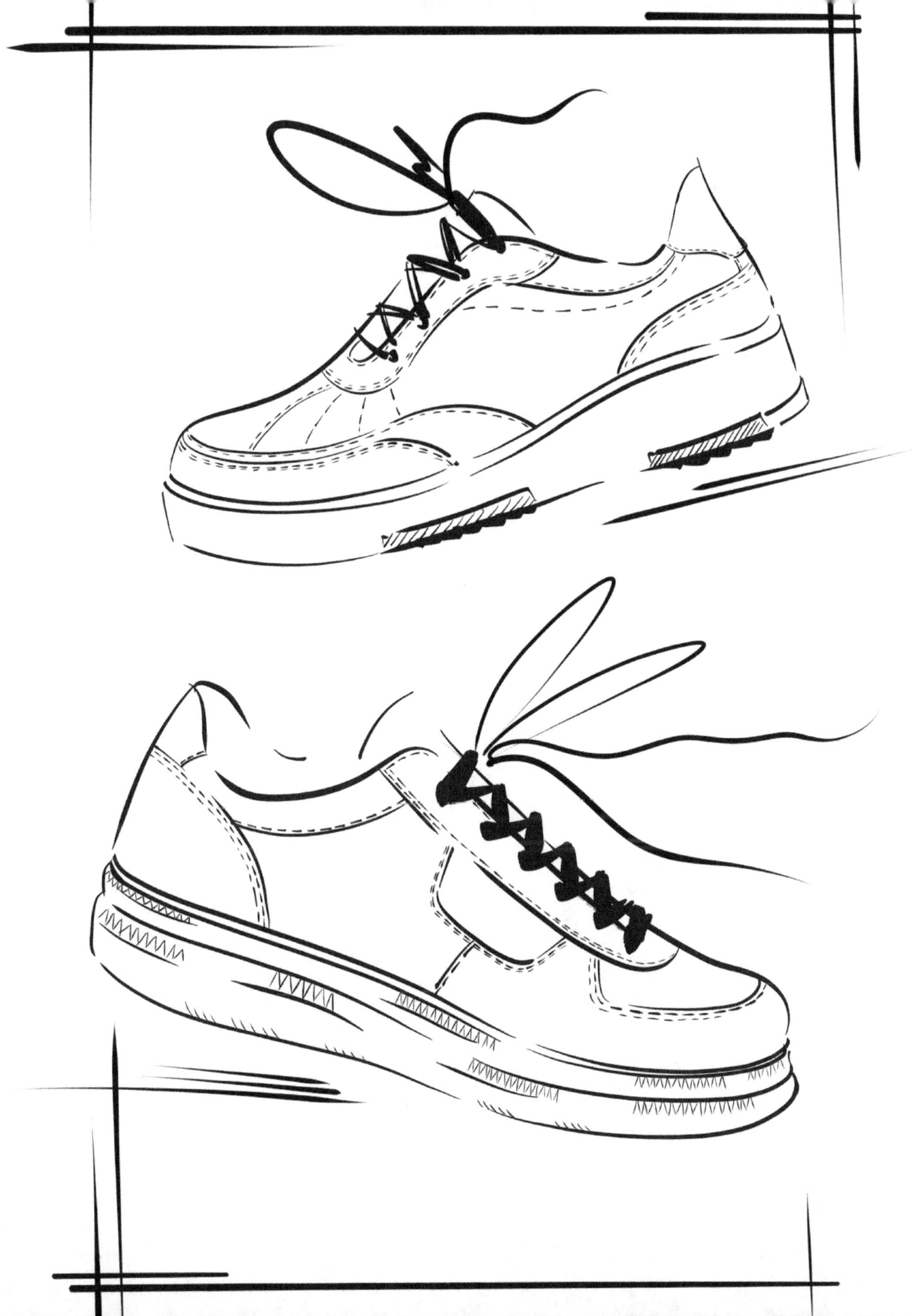

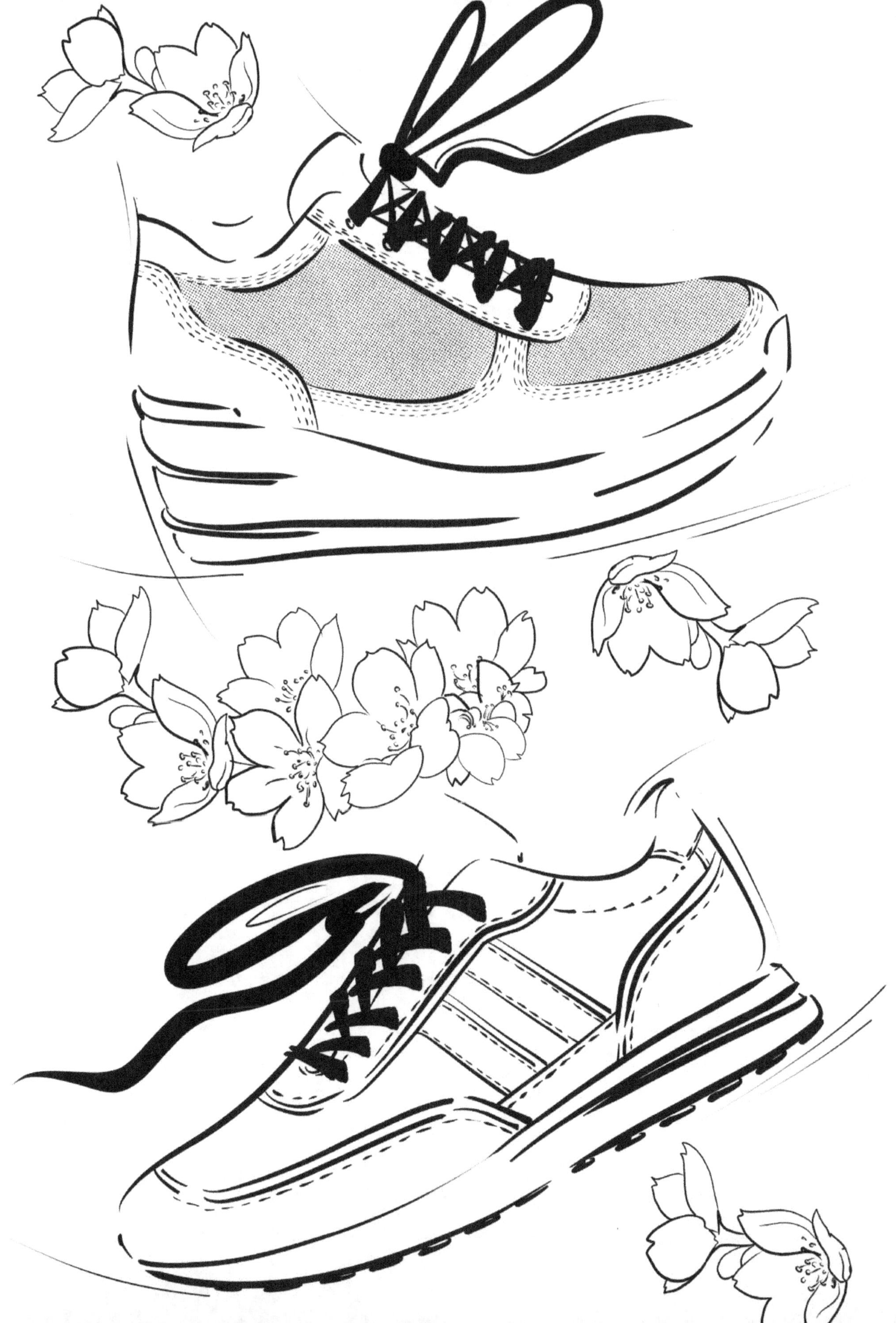

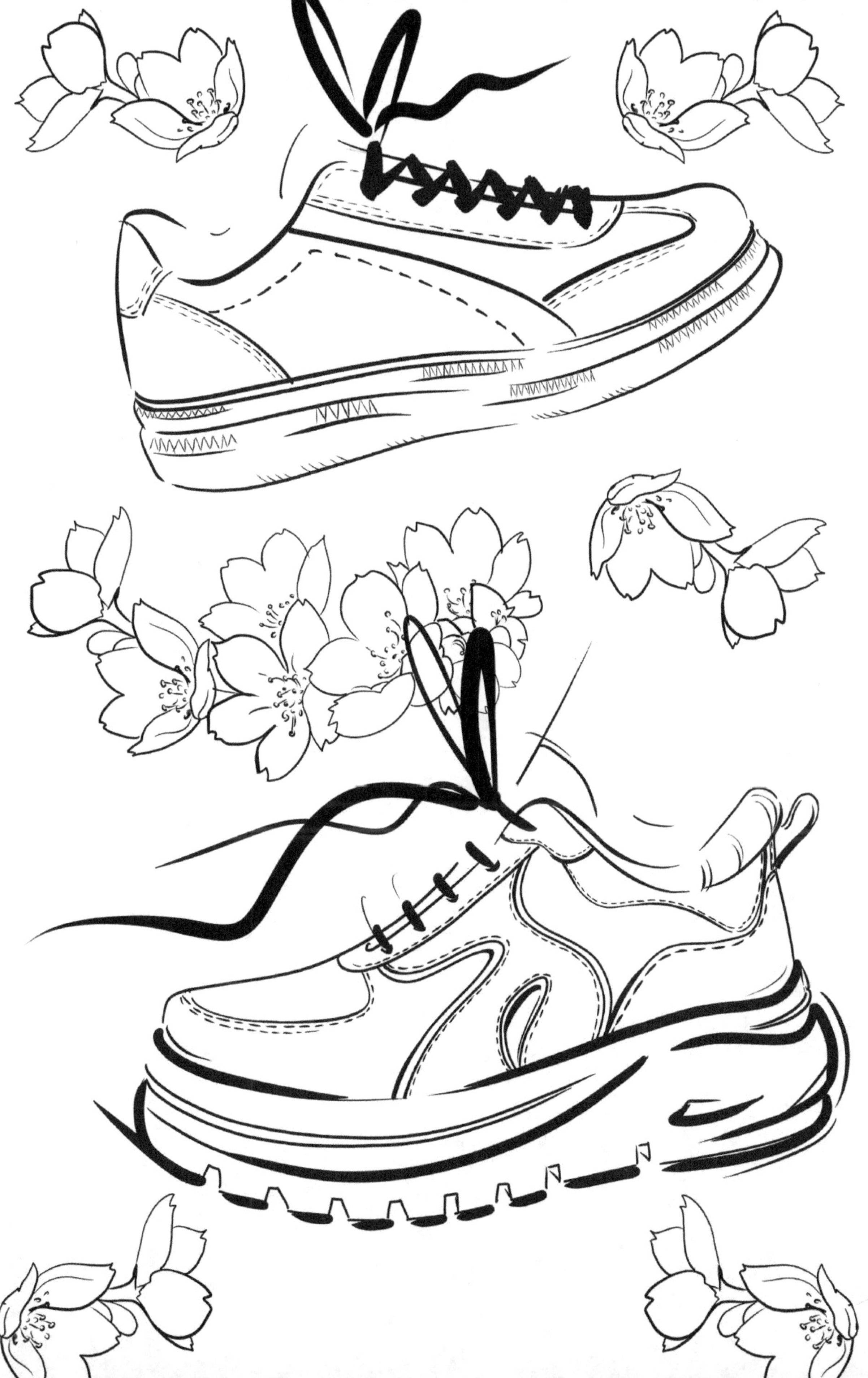

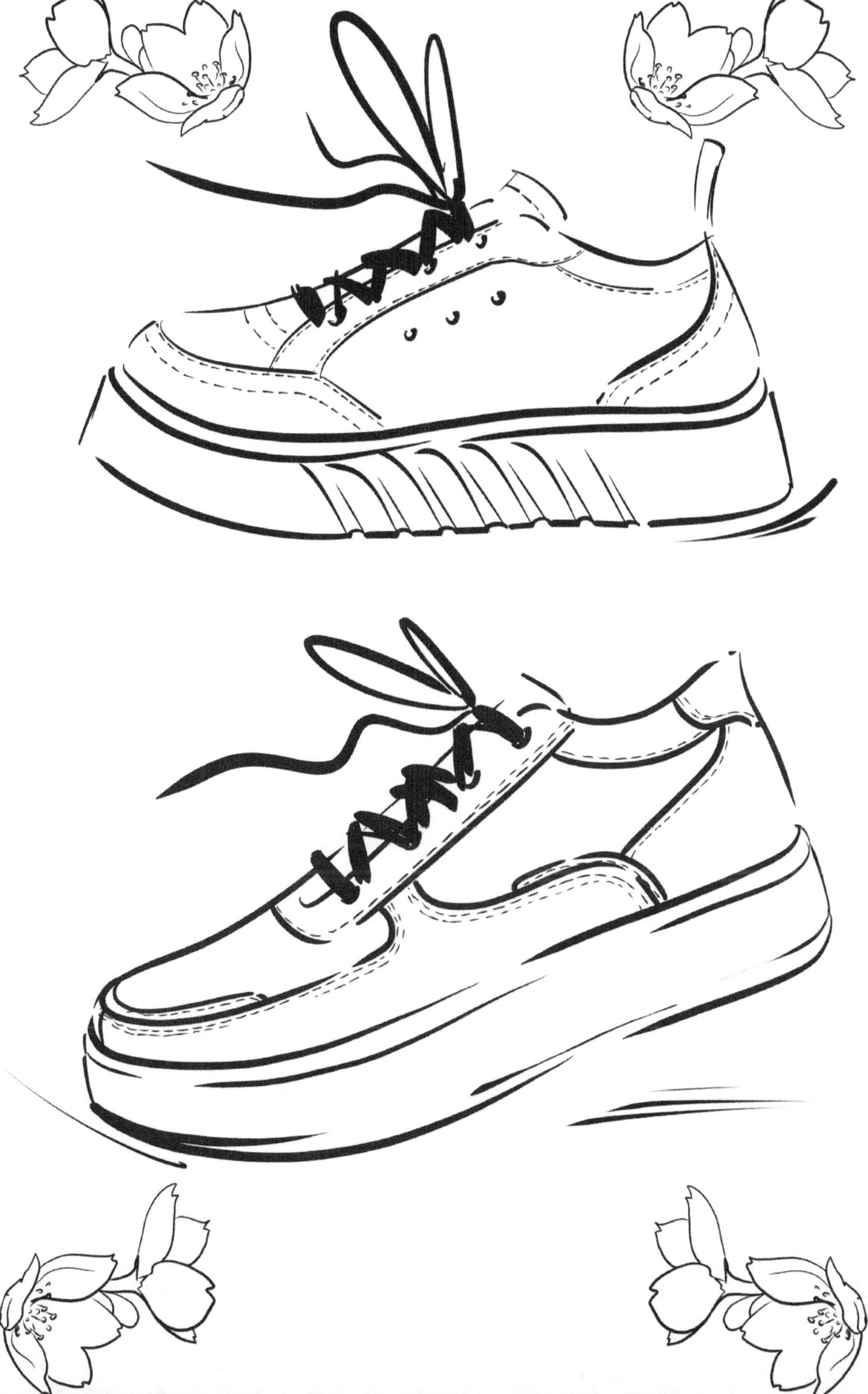

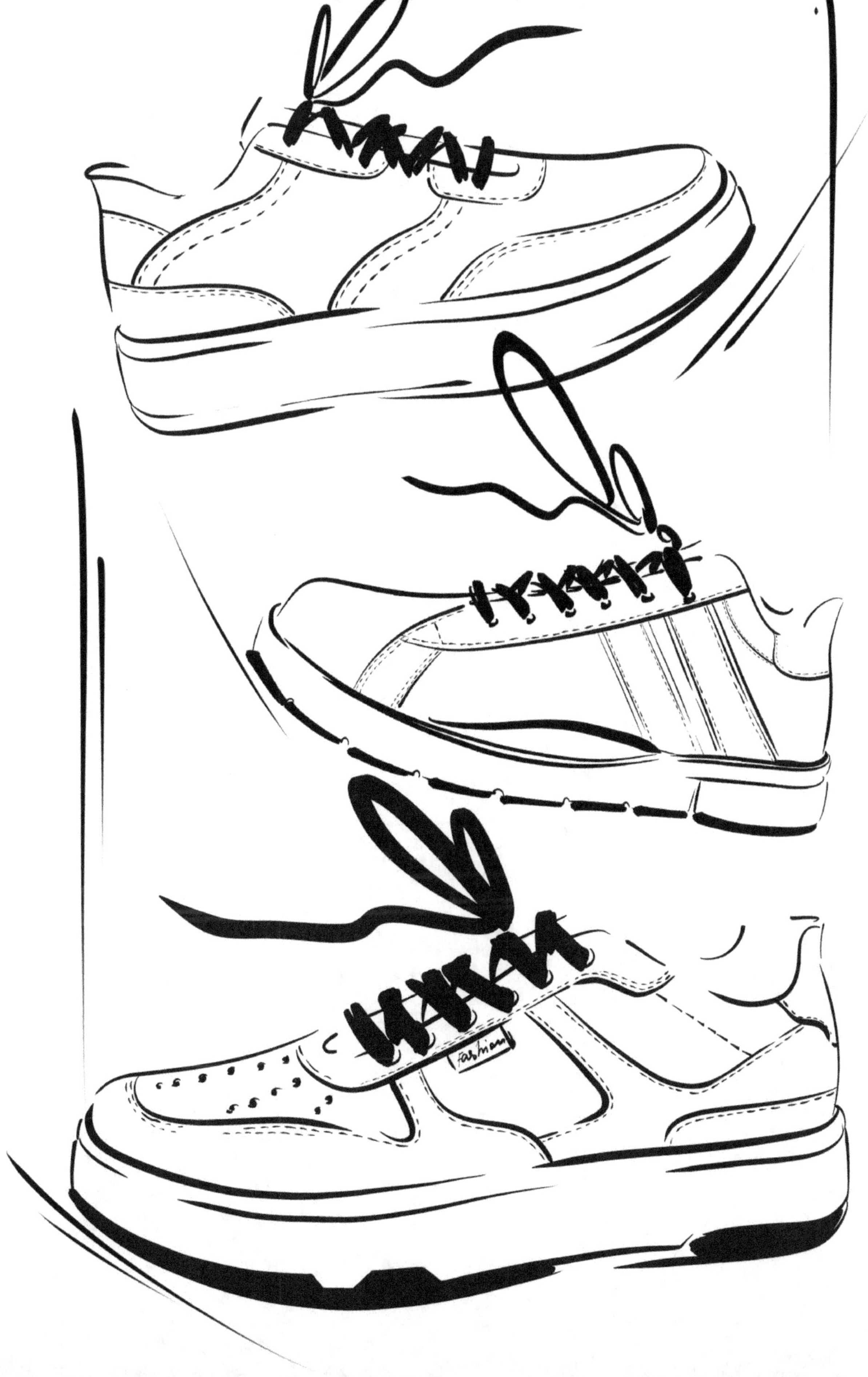

Fashion

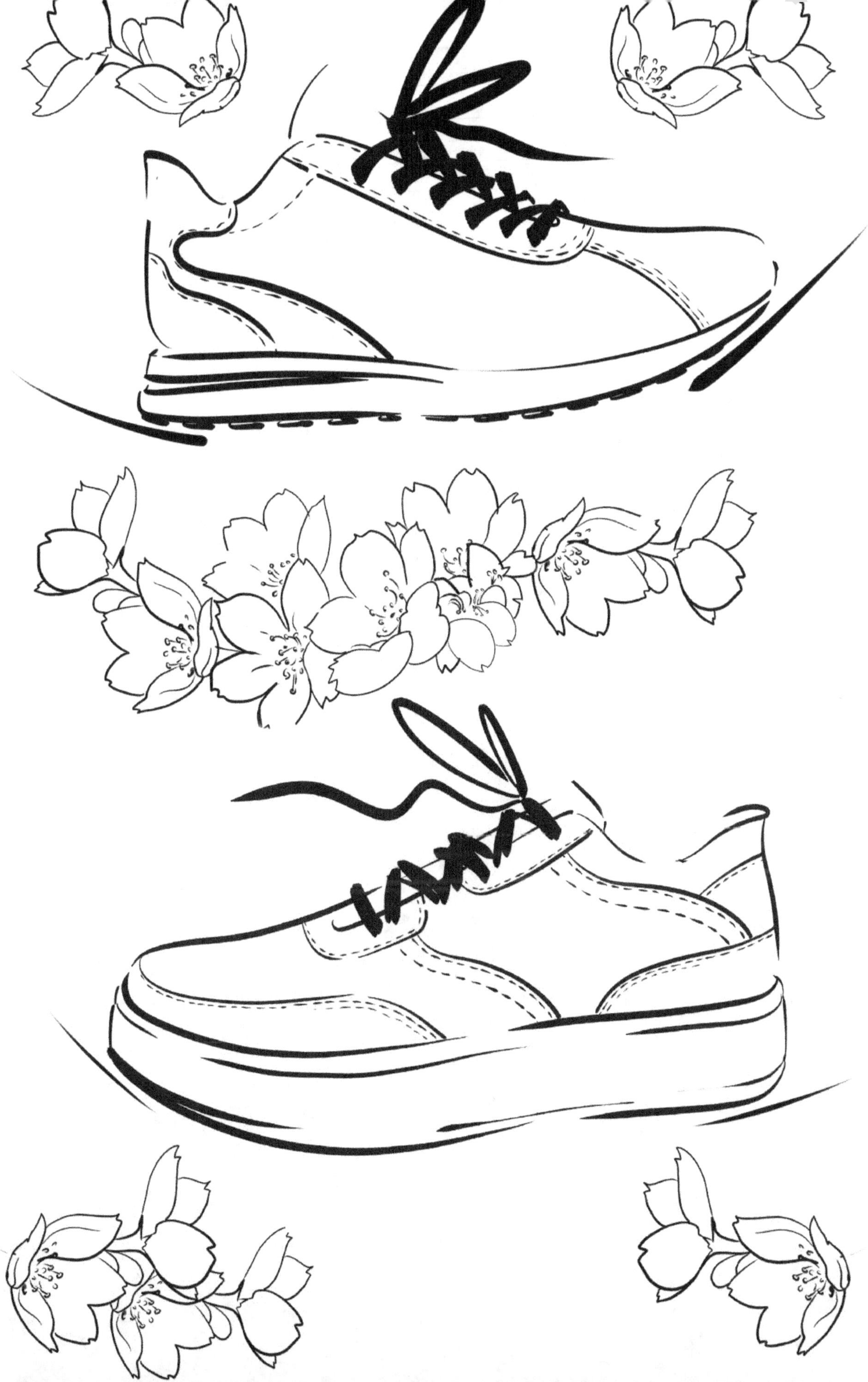

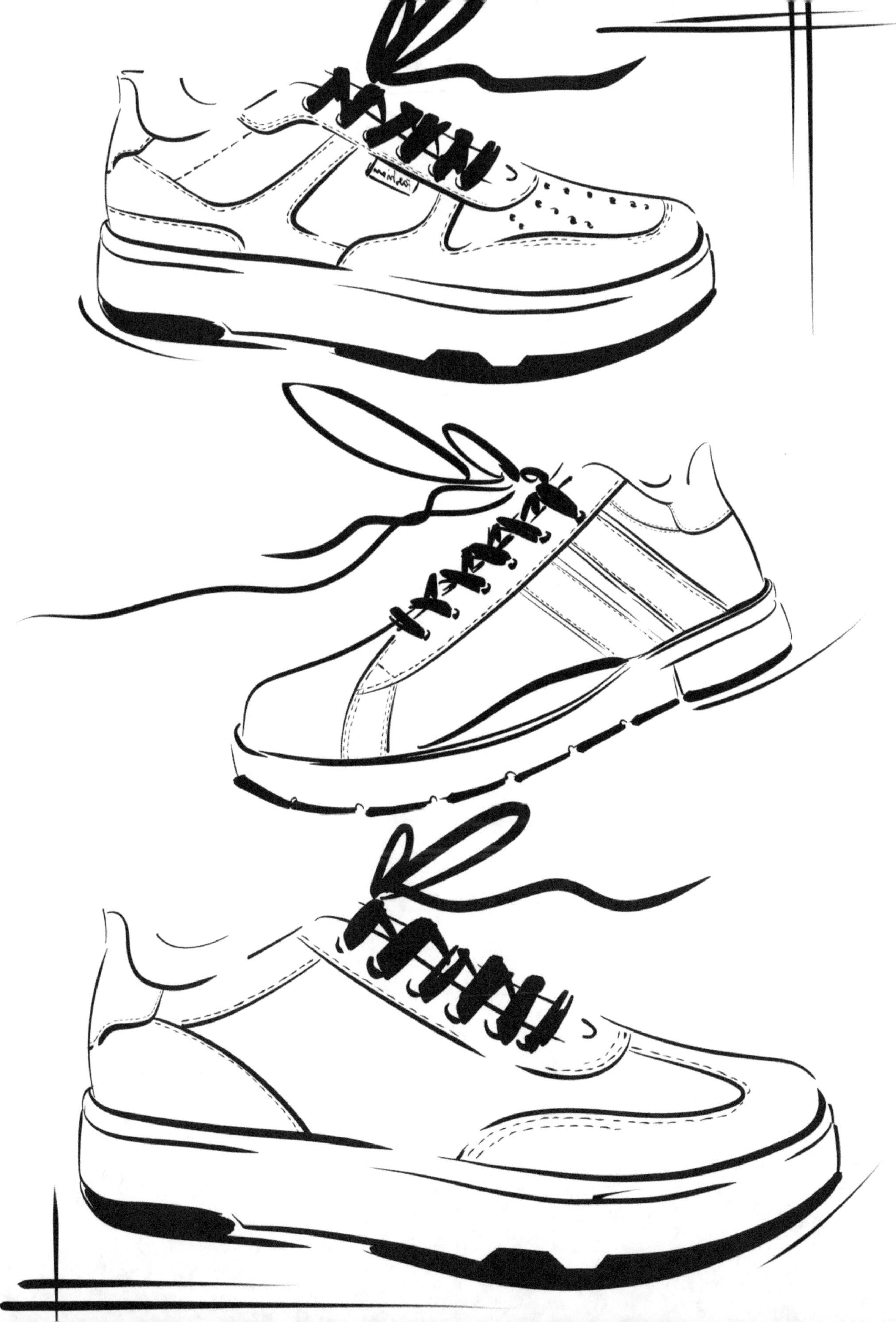

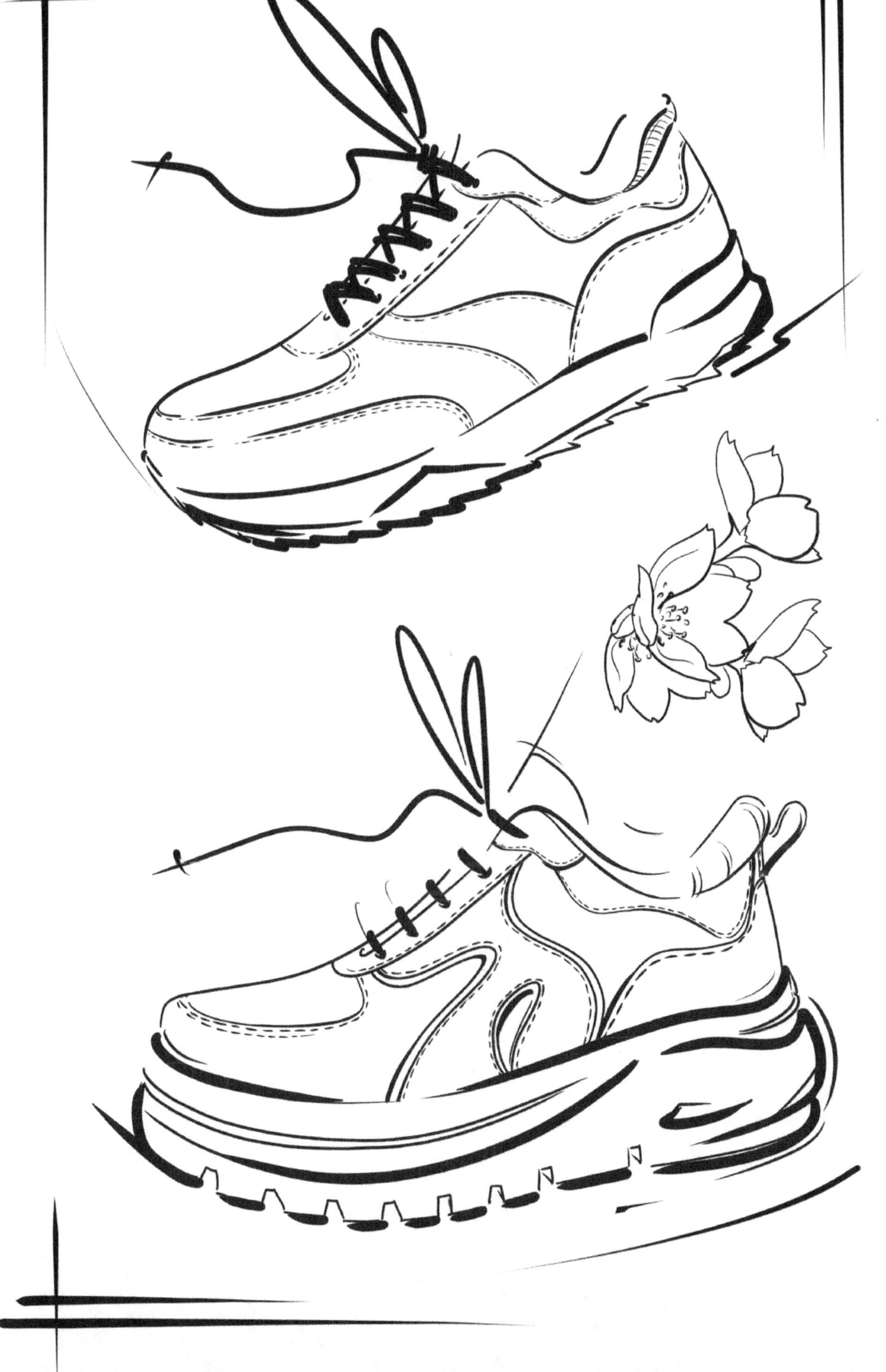

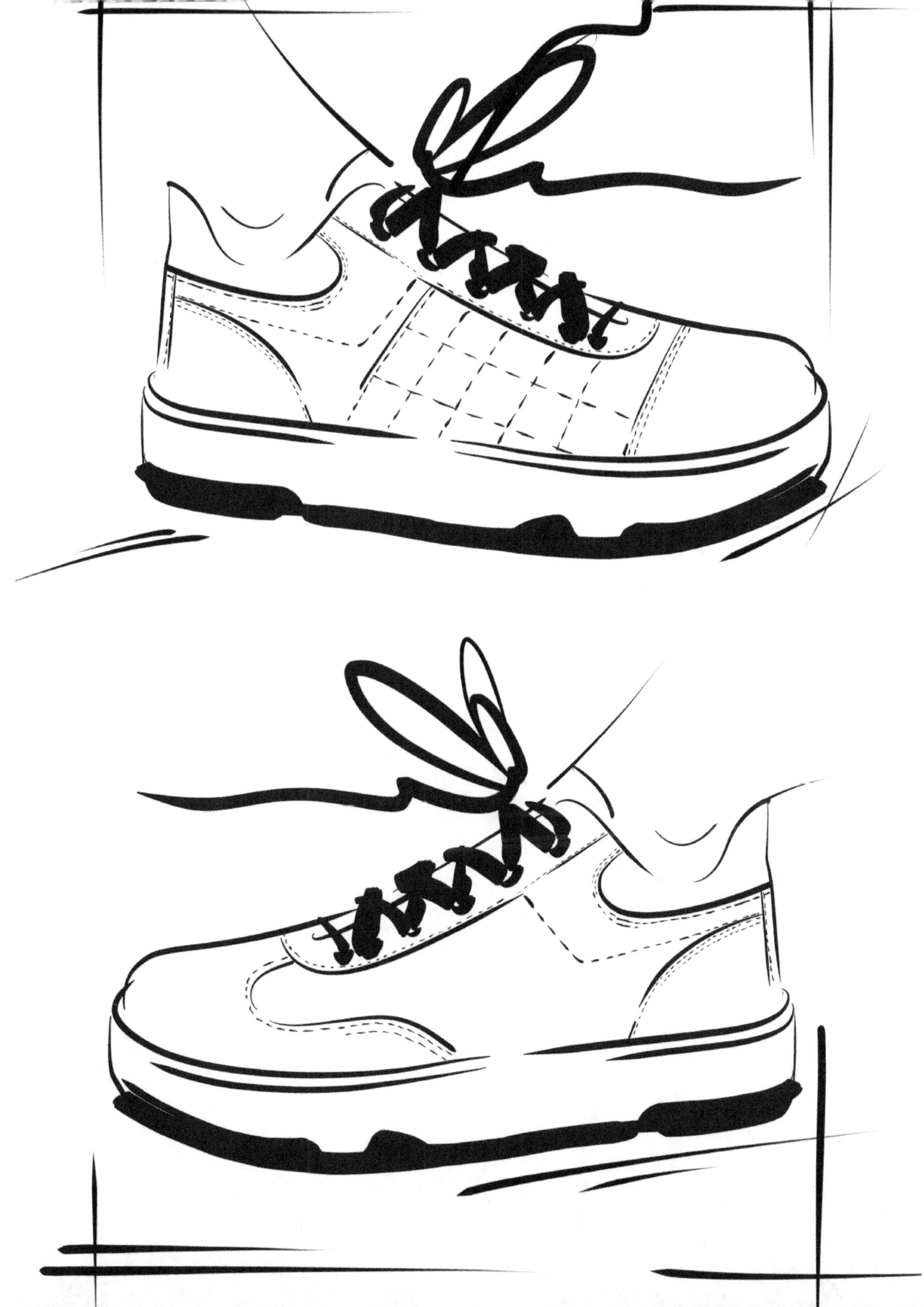

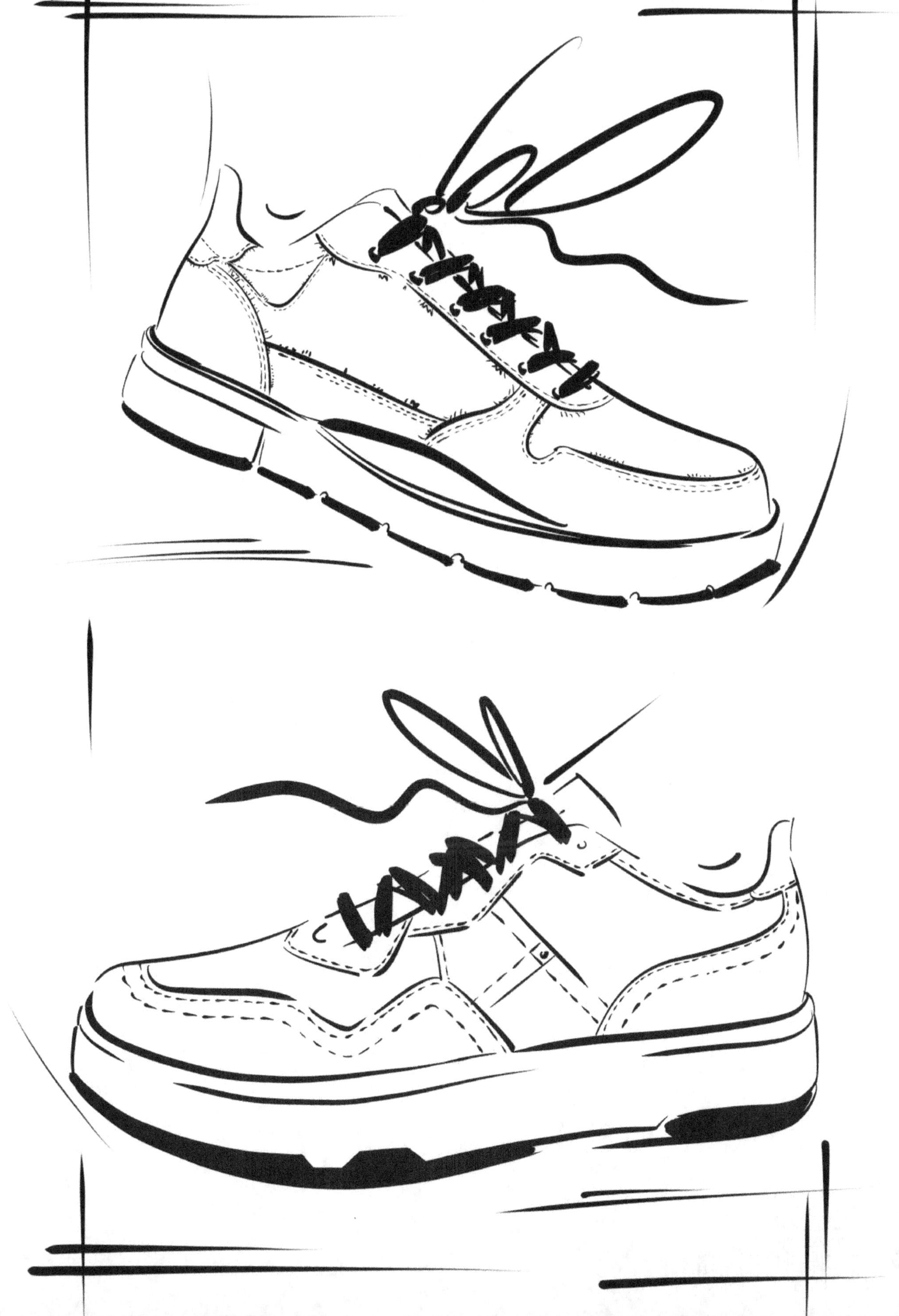